IMOGEN

Adapted from William Shakespeare's *Cymbeline*
by Matthew Dunster

OBERON BOOKS
LONDON

First published in 2016 by Oberon Books Ltd
521 Caledonian Road, London N7 9RH
Tel: +44 (0) 20 7607 3637 / Fax: +44 (0) 20 7607 3629
e-mail: info@oberonbooks.com
www.oberonbooks.com

A catalogue record for this book is available from the British
Library.

PB ISBN: 9781786820471
E ISBN: 9781786820488

Cover:
Background artwork by Dan Hillier
Photography by Owen Harvey

Printed and bound by CPI Group (UK) Ltd, Croydon, CR0 4YY.

Visit www.oberonbooks.com to read more about all our books
and to buy them. You will also find features, author interviews and
news of any author events, and you can sign up for e-newsletters
so that you're always first to hear about our new releases.

For Emma Rice

Acknowledgements

I would like to thank Jon Bausor for grasping hold of my first rough idea, then getting well ahead, to create a world for me to write into.

Thank you, Anastasia Dyson, for the detailed and dogged recording of changes to the script in rehearsal.

It's very important to me to be able to acknowledge the work of Giles Block, Shakespeare's Globe Associate - Text. In previous years, Giles has supported me through edits of *Troilus and Cressida* and *Dr Faustus*; and greatly increased both my understanding and love of Renaissance drama texts. With *Imogen*; as I went further, and both cut more and adapted more, Giles supported me but often challenged me to find better, more sensitive, modern alternatives; and occasionally to revisit and reinstate the Shakespeare. Together, we worked to maintain the integrity of Shakespeare's rhythms (Giles calls it 'the pulse') and meaning. In re-imagining *Cymbeline*, my aim has been to be respectful, but to accept that it is overwritten and not always dramatically successful because of those textual excesses. I wanted to present the audience with what I feel are the most exciting elements of Shakespeare's play; and to further charge that meeting point with some modern tailoring of the wonderful language. Giles was sensitive to the fact that, where I changed words or the structure of speeches, it was only to make sure the poetry and the drama were never obscured by perplexing language or archaic meaning. I am indebted to him for his great knowledge, taste, generosity and patience.

Characters

IMOGEN

POSTHUMUS

CYMBELINE

QUEEN

CLOTEN

CARVILIUS

CORNELIUS

PISANIA

GIACOMO

PHILARIA

FLAVIEN

BELARIUS

CAIUS LUCIUS

GUIDERIUS

ARVIGARIUS

HELEN

Imogen was first performed at the Shakespeare's Globe, London on 5 September 2016 with the following cast:

PISANIA	Leila Ayad
CARVILIUS	Okorie Chukwu
QUEEN	Claire-Louise Cordwell
ARVIRAGUS	William Grint
IMOGEN	Maddy Hill
HELEN	Sapphire Joy
GUIDERIUS	Scott Karim
PHILARIA	Erica Kouassi
CLOTEN	Joshua Lacey
POSTHUMUS	Ira Mandela Siobhan
BELARIUS	Martin Marquez
CYMBELINE	Jonathan McGuinness
CAIUS LUCIUS	Malik-Sankara Mosiah Watson
GIACOMO	Matthew Needham
CORNELIUS	Anwar Russell
FLAVIEN	Kai Spellman

Creative Team	
Director	Matthew Dunster
Designer	Jon Bausor
Choreographer	Christopher Akrill
Lighting Designer	Lee Curran
Sound Designer	George Dennis
Fight Director	RC-Annie Ltd
Costume Supervisor	Tash Prynne
Assistant Director	Nicole Charles
Globe Associate – Text	Giles Block
Globe Associate – Movement	Glynn MacDonald
Voice & Dialect	Martin McKellan
Deputy Text Associate	Christine Schmidle

SCENE ONE

Britain.

CYMBELINE's warehouse.

Everyone onstage.

Everyone in black.

Some music.

We see the drug production that is the 'business' of CYMBELINE's gang. It is chemical and detailed.

One man approaches. This is BELARIUS in disguise. He hands CARVILIUS a bag. Carvilius opens it and takes out large, well packed bags of marijuana leaf. He hands BELARIUS an envelope. BELARIUS opens it – looks at the contents and nods.

A girl walks forward. She wears cool, black, street clothes. BELARIUS checks her out.

CARVILIUS:	Imogen.
BELARIUS:	Innogen?
CARVILIUS:	No – Imogen. Immmm – m – Imogen.
BELARIUS:	But, pray you, tell me, Is she sole child to the king?
CARVILIUS:	His only child.

Music changes.

CARVILIUS goes to a microphone.

He had two sons...

Two boys come on in simple cotton vests and pants.

IMOGEN takes off her top and bottoms to reveal simple cotton vest and pants.

The boys carry balloons and hand one to Imogen.

One of them is deaf. So they sign.

CYMBELINE walks forward. He plays with them all.

He had two sons, who from their nursery
Were stolen, and to this hour no guess in knowledge
Which way they went.

The music changes – it's loud and frightening.

Everyone moves in on the boys. Like a dangerous wave, they take them. Their balloons float away.

The music changes.

IMOGEN left alone.

She signs something – but the signing fades away.

BELARIUS watches the boy's balloons.

BELARIUS: How long is this ago?

CARVILIUS: Some twenty years.

A boy walks forward in simple vest and pants.

He has a balloon tied to his wrist.

CYMBELINE takes his arm and guides him in IMOGEN's direction.

Posthumus.
His father served with glory against the Romans,
And died with his blade in hand. His mother,
Big of this gentleman our theme, deceased
As he was born. The king he takes the babe
To his protection.

The music changes.

IMOGEN and POSTHUMUS play together.

They tie each other's balloons somewhere.

They are dressed by everyone.

Adults now, they are left alone.

They kiss.

CARVILIUS: Whooaahh

BELARIUS: But what's the matter?

CARVILIUS: The king's daughter, and heir of his kingdom, whom
He purposed to his wife's sole son – a widow

QUEEN and CLOTEN walk forward.

That late he married – has wedded herself
Unto this poor but worthy gentleman.

The music changes.

It's loud and frightening.

*Everyone moves in on IMOGEN and POSTHUMUS. Like a dangerous
wave, they take POSTHUMUS.*

IMOGEN is dressed by everyone in prison grey sweatshirt and sweatpants.

Her husband banished; she imprisoned: all
Is outward sorrow; though I think the king
Be touched at very heart.

BELARIUS: None but the king?

CARVILIUS: He that has lost her too; so is the queen,
That most desired the match; but not a courtier,
Although they wear their faces to the bent
Of the king's looks, has a heart that is not
Glad at the thing they scowl at.

BELARIUS: And why so?

CARVILIUS: He that has missed Imogen is a thing
Too bad for bad report: and he that has her –

WOMEN: Whoooahhh

CARVILIUS: I mean, that married her – is a creature such
As, to seek through the regions of the earth
For one his like, there would be something failing
In him that should compare.

BELARIUS: You speak him far.

CARVILIUS: Imogen...
For whom he now is banished, her own price
Proclaims how she esteemed him and his virtue.
By her election may be truly read
What kind of man he is.

SCENE TWO

CYMBELINE's warehouse.

Two rooms.

In one; POSTHUMUS has his expensive looking tracksuit stripped from him. He is given grey sweatpants and sweatshirt.

In the other; IMOGEN sits on the floor while QUEEN stands.

QUEEN: No, be assured you shall not find me, daughter,
                Evil-eyed unto you. You're my prisoner, but
                Your jailer shall deliver you the keys
                That lock up your restraint.

                She makes a sign at the door and POSTHUMUS is pushed in. IMOGEN leaps up and they hold and cling to each other.

                            For you, Posthumus,
                So soon as I can win the offended king,
                I will be known your advocate. Currently
                The fire of rage is in him, and were good
                You leaned toward his sentence. You know the peril.

POSTHUMUS: I leave today.

QUEEN: I'll give you time.

                She leaves.

POSTHUMUS: Do not trust her.

IMOGEN: I hate how that tyrant
                Can tickle where she wounds! My dearest husband,
                You must be gone!

                They look at each other. The horror is dawning.

                And I shall here abide the hourly shot
                Of angry eyes: not comforted to live,
                But that there is this jewel in the world
                That I may see again.

POSTHUMUS: I will remain
                The loyalist husband that did ever swear.

                They kiss; it is passionate, deep, sexual, full of need.
                They break.

My residence in Rome – at one Philaria's,
Daughter to my father's friend – there, write me.

QUEEN comes back in.

QUEEN: Be brief, I pray you:
If the king come, I shall incur I know not
How much of his displeasure.

She leaves.

IMOGEN: Look here, love;
This diamond was my mother's. Take it, heart;
But keep it till you woo another wife,
When Imogen is dead.

He grabs her by the shoulders.

POSTHUMUS: How? How another?

He puts on the ring.

Remain, remain you here. For my sake wear this;

He takes off his bracelet.

It is a manacle of love; I'll place it
Upon this fairest prisoner.

He puts it around her wrist.

IMOGEN: Posthumus,
When shall we see again?

CYMBELINE enters with CARVILIUS and CORNELIUS.

CYMBELINE: You – basest thing – be gone – now – from my sight.
If after this command you fraught the court
With your unworthiness, you die. Away.
You are poison to my blood.

POSTHUMUS: May God protect you,
And bless the good remainders of the court.
I am gone.

He is escorted away by CARVILIUS and CORNELIUS.

IMOGEN: There cannot be a pinch in death
More sharp than this is.

CYMBELINE: You disloyal thing.

IMOGEN:	Harm not yourself with your vexation I am senseless of your wrath; a feeling more rare Subdues all pangs all fears.
CYMBELINE:	Past grace? Obedience?
IMOGEN:	Past hope, and in despair; that way, past grace.
CYMBELINE:	That might have had the sole son of my queen!
IMOGEN:	It is your fault that I have loved Posthumus: You bred him as my playmate, and he is A man worth any woman. *QUEEN comes in.*
CYMBELINE:	Are you mad?
IMOGEN:	Almost! Heaven restore me!
CYMBELINE:	Foolish thing. They were again together. Now pen her up.
QUEEN:	Peace, sweet Cymbeline. Leave us to ourselves.
CYMBELINE:	Let her languish a drop of blood a day; And, being aged, die of this folly! *CYMBELINE leaves.*
QUEEN:	Imogen! You must give way! *QUEEN exits.*

SCENE THREE

POSTHUMUS and CLOTEN fight.

CLOTEN tries hard but POSTHUMUS easily dodges all he can throw at him.

POSTHUMUS does the minimum to overpower CLOTEN.

They are separated.

PISANIA pulls POSTHUMUS away. They exit.

CARVILIUS and CORNELIUS pick up CLOTEN.

CLOTEN:	There's blood on my shirt. Have I hurt him?
CARVILIUS:	Hurt him?
CLOTEN:	The villain would not stand.
CORNELIUS:	Yes – but he ran forward – toward your face.

CLOTEN grabs CORNELIUS violently.

CLOTEN: Would you had not come between us.

He throws CORNELIUS away.

And that she should love him and refuse me!

CARVILIUS: Cloten – as I told you always, her beauty and her brain go not together.

CLOTEN: Would there had been some hurt done! Come, let's go together.

They leave.

SCENE FOUR

IMOGEN's room. CYMBELINE's guards at the door.

IMOGEN: What was the last that he said to you?

PISANIA: It was his Imogen!

IMOGEN: Then waved his hand?

PISANIA: And kissed it.

IMOGEN: And that was all?

PISANIA: For so long as he could make me with this eye,
Distinguish him from others, he waved still.

IMOGEN: Before you left him you should have eye'd him,
As little as a crow.

She takes POSTHUMUS' balloon from earlier and lets it go.

PISANIA: Imogen, I did.

IMOGEN watches the balloon through the following.

IMOGEN: I would have broke mine eye-strings; cracked them, just
To look upon him, till the diminution
Of space had pointed him sharp as a needle,
No, followed him, till he had melted from
The smallness of a gnat to air, and then
Have turned mine eyes and wept. But, good Pisania,
When shall we hear from him?

PISANIA: Be assured,
At his first opportunity.

During the following speech POSTHUMUS *appears by* IMOGEN'S *side. There are echoes of the material from Scene 1: them meeting, kissing each other etc.*

IMOGEN: I did not take my leave of him, but had
Most pretty things to say: before I could tell him
How I would think on him at certain hours
Such thoughts and such, or I could make him swear
The shes of Italy should not betray
Mine interest and his honour, or have charged him,
At the sixth hour of morn, at noon, at midnight,
To meet my prayers with prayers, for then
I am in heaven for him; or before I could
Give him that parting kiss, comes in my father!

The dangerous wave takes POSTHUMUS *away.*

HELEN enters.

HELEN: The queen, desires your company.

IMOGEN: *(To* PISANIA.*)* These things I bid you do. Get them dispatched.

SCENE FIVE

Rome.

PHILARIA's home.

Everyone is in white.

There are fans everywhere.

PHILARIA: You don't know what you're talking about!

GIACOMO: Believe it – I have seen him in Britain – but I looked on him then without the help of admiration.

PHILARIA: Nah – nah.

FLAVIEN: I have seen him in France: we had very many there could behold the sun with as firm eyes as he.

PHILARIA: You speak of him when he was less furnished than now he is.

GIACOMO:	This matter of marrying his king's daughter? Wherein he must be weighed rather by her value than his own? And *then* his *banishment*.
	He laughs.
	But how comes it he is to sojourn with you? How creeps acquaintance?
PHILARIA:	His father and mine were soldiers together. Here comes the Briton: let him be so entertained as suits men of your knowing to a stranger of his quality.
	POSTHUMUS enters.
	I ask you to be better known to this gentleman; whom I commend to you as a noble friend of mine.
FLAVIEN:	We have known together in Orleans.
POSTHUMUS:	Since when I have been debtor to you.
FLAVIEN:	I was glad I did atone my countryman and you. It had been pity you fought with so mortal a purpose, upon something so slight.
GIACOMO:	Can we ask what was the difference?
FLAVIEN:	It was an argument where each of them fell in praise of their country's women.
PHILARIA:	What?
FLAVIEN:	Posthumus at that time vouching his to be more fair, virtuous, wise, and less attemptable than any of the rarest of our ladies in France.
GIACOMO:	You mean *as* fair and *as* good – a kind of hand in hand comparison.
POSTHUMUS:	Nah.
GIACOMO:	You must not so far prefer her to ours of Rome?
POSTHUMUS:	I would.
GIACOMO:	If she went before others I have seen, as that diamond of yours outlustres many I have beheld, I could believe she excelled many; but I have not seen the *most* precious diamond there is, nor you the lady.
POSTHUMUS:	I praise her as I rate her; so do I my stone.

GIACOMO:	What do you esteem it at?
POSTHUMUS:	More than the world enjoys.
GIACOMO:	Either your unparagoned mistress is dead, or she's outprized by a trifle.
POSTHUMUS:	You're mistaken. One may be sold, or given, if there were wealth enough for the purchase, or merit for the gift; the other is not a thing for sale, and only a gift of God.
GIACOMO:	Which God had given you?

POSTHUMUS opens his arms and smiles.

	But you know strange fowl light upon neighbouring ponds. Your ring may be stolen too. A cunning thief might hazard the winning of both.
POSTHUMUS:	Your Rome contains none so accomplished to unlock the honour of my wife.
PHILARIA:	Let us leave here –
GIACOMO:	I could get ground of her.
POSTHUMUS:	Nah, nah.
GIACOMO:	I dare gamble half my estate against your ring; which, in my opinion, overvalues it something. But I make my wager rather against your confidence than her reputation.
FLAVIEN:	Enough of this –
PHILARIA:	It came in too suddenly let it die as it was born.
GIACOMO:	I will lay you ten thousand to your ring. Commend me to where your lady is, and I will bring from there that honour of hers, which you imagine so reserved.
POSTHUMUS:	I will wage money against your money. My ring I hold dear as my finger; it's part of it.
GIACOMO:	You are afraid I would undergo what's spoken.
POSTHUMUS:	Will you?

Silence.

Standoff.

I shall lend my diamond till your return. My wife exceeds in goodness the hugeness of your unworthy thinking. I dare you. Here's my ring.

PHILARIA:	I will not have this.
GIACOMO:	If I bring you no sufficient testimony that I have enjoyed the dearest bodily part of your wife: she, your jewel; this, your jewel; and my money are yours.
POSTHUMUS:	And if she remain unseduced, for your ill opinion and the assault you've made on her you shall answer me with your blade.
GIACOMO:	Agreed. I will fetch the money. Your hand.
	They shake hands.

SCENE SIX

A room in CYMBELINE's warehouse.

QUEEN:	Now, master doctor, have you brought those drugs?
	CORNELIUS produces a small box.
CORNELIUS:	My conscience bids me ask wherefore you have Commanded of me those most poisonous compounds, Which are the movers of a languishing death; But though slow, deadly?
QUEEN:	I wonder, doctor, You ask me such a question. Have I not been Your pupil long? Have you not learn'd me how To make perfumes? Distil? Preserve? Yes, so That our great king himself does often woo me For my confections? Having so far proceeded – Unless you think me devilish – is it not meet That I did amplify my judgment in Other conclusions? I will try the forces Of these your compounds on such creatures as We count not worth the hanging – but none human – To try the vigour of them and apply Antidotes to their act, and by them gather Their several virtues and effects.
CORNELIUS:	You, Shall from this practise just make hard your heart!
QUEEN:	O, be quiet.

PISANIA comes in.

                              How now, Pisania?
Doctor, your service for this time is ended.

CORNELIUS: *(Aside.)* I do suspect you, madam;
            But you shall do no harm.

QUEEN: *(To PISANIA.)* Come here, a word.

            They move to view IMOGEN.

CORNELIUS: I do not like her. I do know her spirit,
            And will not trust one of her malice with
            A drug of such damned nature. That she has
            Will stupefy and dull the sense awhile;
            No danger in what show of death it makes,
            More than the locking-up the spirits a time,
            To be more fresh, reviving. She is fooled
            With a most false effect; and I the truer,
            So to be false with her.

            He leaves.

            *QUEEN and PISANIA watch IMOGEN. IMOGEN is sat with her head
            between her knees.*

QUEEN: Do you think in time
            She will not cool and let instructions enter
            Where folly now possesses? Do your work.
            Show your good friend her advantage with my son.
            When you do bring me word that she loves him,
            I'll tell you on the instant you are then
            As great as is Posthumus, greater, for
            His fortunes all lie speechless and his name
            Is at last gasp. Return he cannot, nor
            Continue where he is. What can you hope for,
            To be depender on a thing that leans,
            Who cannot be new built, nor has no friends,
            So much as but to prop him?

            QUEEN offers PISANIA the box.

            It is a thing I made, which has the king
            Five times redeemed from death. Please, you take it –

It is a foretaste of a further good
That I mean to you.

PISANIA reaches for the box – so they are both holding it now.

                    Tell Imogen how
The case stands with her. Do it as from yourself.
She will take notice of you. I'll move the king
To any shape of your preferment such
As you desire. Fare you well, Pisania.
Think on my words.

PISANIA leaves.

                    A sly and constant girl,
Not to be shaked. The agent for Posthumus;
And reminder to our daughter to hold
Her marriage to that man. I've given her that, which,
When taken, shall quite unpeople Imogen
Of ambassadors from her sweet. And which,
Unless she mend her humour, she'll be assured
To taste of too.

SCENE SEVEN

Music.

We see POSTHUMUS in Rome – handing over letters to GIACOMO.

We see IMOGEN in Britain – her daily visits from her father, QUEEN and CLOTEN.

SCENE EIGHT

IMOGEN in her room, reading from a letter.

GIACOMO and PISANIA watching.

IMOGEN: 'He is one of the noblest note, to whose kindnesses I am
            most infinitely tied. Reflect upon him accordingly, as
            you value your trust…'

            IMOGEN looks at PISANIA and GIACOMO.

            So far I read aloud –

PISANIA: Read it!

The women laugh.

PISANIA goes out.

IMOGEN goes on to her knees and reads the rest of the letter to herself.

GIACOMO: *(Aside.)* All of her that is out of door is most rich.
If she be furnished with a mind so rare,
I've lost the wager. Boldness be my friend.
Arm me, audacity, from head to foot.

IMOGEN lets out a massive sigh.

IMOGEN: But even the very middle of my heart
Is warmed by the rest, and takes it thankfully.
You are as welcome, Giacomo, as I
Have words to bid you, and shall find it so
In all that I can do.

GIACOMO: Thanks, fairest lady.
What, are men mad? Has nature given them eyes
To see this vaulted sky, and the rich scope
Of sea and land, and can we not distinguish
Between fair and foul?

IMOGEN: What makes your amazement?

GIACOMO: It cannot be in the eye, for apes and monkeys
Between two such women would chatter for one,
Condemn with frowns the other; nor in the judgment,
For idiots in this case of favour would
Be wisely definite.

IMOGEN: What, raps you? Are you well?

PISANIA returns with beers for all. GIACOMO takes one.

GIACOMO: Thanks – very well.

                    (To PISANIA.)   Pisania?

PISANIA: Yes.

GIACOMO: Please find
My man's abode, where I did leave him, and
Give him welcome.

PISANIA leaves.

IMOGEN: Posthumus is well?

GIACOMO: He is well; is well.

IMOGEN: Is he disposed to mirth? I hope he is.

GIACOMO: Exceeding pleasant; not a stranger there
           So merry and so gamesome. He is called
           The Briton Reveller.

IMOGEN: When he was here,
           He did incline to sadness, and often
           Not knowing why.

GIACOMO: I never saw him sad.
           There's a Frenchman, his companion, who much loves
           A girl he left at home; he furnaces
           The thick sighs from him, whiles the jolly Briton –
           Posthumus – laughs from his free lungs, cries 'O,
           Can my sides hold, to think that man, who knows
           What woman is, yes, what she cannot choose
           But must be, will waste his free hours away from
           Married bondage?'

IMOGEN: He says that?

GIACOMO: It is a recreation to be by
           And hear him mock the Frenchman. But, heaven knows,
           Some men are much to blame.

IMOGEN: Not he, I hope.

GIACOMO: Not he. But yet – heaven's bounty towards him might
           Be used more thankfully: in himself, it is much;
           In you, which I account his, beyond all talents.

           He looks at her.

           Whilst I am bound to wonder, I am bound
           To pity too.

IMOGEN: What do you pity?

GIACOMO: Two creatures.

IMOGEN: Am I one?

           GIACOMO looks down.

           Why do you pity me?

GIACOMO: That others do –

           A beat.

           I was about to say enjoy your – but

It's not mine to speak of –

IMOGEN: You seem to know
Something of me, or what concerns me. Please
Discover to me what both you spur and stop.

GIACOMO: Had I this cheek
To bathe my lips upon; this hand, whose touch,
Whose every touch, would force the feeler's soul
To the oath of loyalty; if I should then,
Slaver with common lips; grip other's hands
Made hard with hourly falsehood – it were fit
That all the plagues of hell should at one time
Encounter such revolt.

IMOGEN: So my husband
Has forgot Britain.

GIACOMO: I did not want
To pronounce the beggary of his change;
But your graces do charm this report out.

IMOGEN: Let me hear no more.

GIACOMO: O, Imogen, your cause does strike my heart
With pity, that makes me sick. Be revenged;
Or she that bore you was no queen!

IMOGEN: Revenged!
How should I be revenged? If this be true –
As I have such a heart that both mine ears
Must not in haste abuse – if it be true,
How should I be revenged?

GIACOMO: Should he make you
Live, like a chaste nun between cold sheets,
Whiles he is straddling numerous whores,
In your despite, upon your purse? Revenge it.
I dedicate myself to your sweet pleasure,
More noble than that betrayer to your bed.

IMOGEN: Pisania!

GIACOMO: Let me my service tender on your lips.

IMOGEN: Away! I do condemn mine ears that have
So long attended you. If you were honourable,

You would have told this tale for virtue, not
For such an end you seek – as base as strange.
You do wrong Posthumus who is as far
From your report as you from honour, and
Solicit here a woman that disdains
You and the devil alike. Come here, Pisania!
The king my father shall be made acquainted
Of your assault. If he shall think it fit,
A saucy stranger in his court expound
His beastly mind to us, he has a court
He little cares for and a daughter who
He not respects at all. Pisania!

GIACOMO: Happy Posthumus. Give me your pardon.
I have spoke this, to know if your faithfulness
Were deeply rooted. Please be not angry,
Mighty Imogen, that I have adventured
To test your taking of a false report, which has
Honoured with confirmation your great judgment
In the election of a man so rare,
He sits 'mongst men like a descended god.
He has a kind of honour sets him off,
More than a mortal seeming.

IMOGEN: You make amends.

GIACOMO: The love I bear him made me stir you so,
But God made you unlike all others. Pardon.

IMOGEN: All's well. Take my power in the court for yours.

GIACOMO: My humble thanks. I had almost forgot –
I have a small request, but it concerns
Posthumus; he and other noble friends,
Are partners in the business.

IMOGEN: What is it?

GIACOMO: Some dozen of us have mingled our sums
To buy a present for the emperor
Which I, the factor for the rest, have done
In France. They're plates of rare design, and jewels
Of rich and exquisite form. Their values great,
And I am anxious being a stranger,

	To have them in safe stowage. May it please you To take them in protection?
IMOGEN:	Willingly; Since my husband has an interest in them, I will keep them in my bedchamber.
GIACOMO:	They are in a trunk, Attended by my men. I will make bold To send them to you, only for this night; I must away to-morrow.
IMOGEN:	O, no, no.
GIACOMO:	Yes.
IMOGEN:	Not away tomorrow.
GIACOMO:	Yes, I must. Therefore, if you wish, to greet Posthumus With writing, do it tonight.
IMOGEN:	I will write.

He begins to leave.

Send your trunk to me; it shall safe be kept
And faithfully returned.

SCENE NINE

CLOTEN beats someone while CARVILIUS and CORNELIUS watch.

The 'someone' crawls, then stands, then staggers away.

CLOTEN:	Whoreson dog! I gave him satisfaction. I had rather not be so noble as I am. They dare not fight with me, because of the queen my mother, and I must go up and down like a cock that nobody can match.
CORNELIUS:	Like a cock.
	CLOTEN looks at him.
	That nobody can match.
CARVILIUS:	Did you hear of a stranger that's come to court tonight?
CLOTEN:	A stranger

CARVELIUS:	There's a Roman come; and, it's thought, one of Posthumus' friends.
CLOTEN:	Posthumus! A banished rascal! And he's another, whatsoever he be; come, I'll go see this Roman. What I have lost today I'll win tonight of him. Come, go.

SCENE TEN

IMOGEN's room.

A large bag in one corner.

IMOGEN reading in bed.

IMOGEN:	Helen?
HELEN:	Imogen.
IMOGEN:	What hour is it?
HELEN:	Almost midnight.
IMOGEN:	I have read three hours then. My eyes are weak.
	She kisses the bracelet on her arm
	Wake me in the morning.
	HELEN leaves.
	Sleep has seized me wholly.
	IMOGEN goes to sleep.
	We watch.
	The bag starts to unzip and GIACOMO sticks his head out.
	He climbs out.
	He stretches.
	He goes to the bed.
	He stares down at IMOGEN.
	We hear his thoughts in voice over.
GIACOMO:	How bravely you become your bed, fresh lily, And whiter than the sheets! That I might touch! But kiss; one kiss! Rubies unparagon'd, How dearly they do it! It's her breathing

25

That perfumes the chamber so. But my design:
To note the chamber. I will write all down.

He writes in his notebook.

Such and such pictures; there the window; such
The adornment of her bed; such and such.

He trails off, bored of such details.

Ah, but some natural marks about her body,
Would enrich my testimony.

She stirs.

O sleep, you ape of death, lie dull upon her!
And be her sense but as a monument,
That's in a chapel lying!

He begins to slide her bracelet off.

                                        Come off, come off.
It is mine. And this will witness strongly,
To the madding of her lord.

He lifts the sheets to look at her half-naked body.

                                     On her left breast
A mole like a drop of crimson. This secret
Will force him think I have picked the lock and taken
The treasure of her honour. No more. To what end?
Why should I write this down, that's riveted,
Screw'd to my memory? I have enough.
To the trunk again.

He climbs into the bag.

                                 I lodge in fear;
Though this a heavenly angel, hell is here.

He zips up the bag.

SCENE ELEVEN

CLOTEN outside IMOGEN's room with a boombox. CARVILIUS and CORNELIUS are with him.

CLOTEN: I am advised to give her music in the mornings, they say
                it will penetrate.

He presses play.

Music.

HELEN walks by CLOTEN and shakes her head at him.

She enters IMOGEN's room and throws some clothes at her.

IMOGEN dresses.

Outside – CLOTEN is weirdly kind of playing air-guitar.

If this music can penetrate her with it's fingering – so.
I'll try with tongue too. If none will do, let her remain.
But I'll never give over.

CARVILIUS: Here comes the king.

CYMBELINE and QUEEN approach.

CYMBELINE: Attend you here the door of our stern daughter?
Will she not forth?

CLOTEN: I have assailed her with music, but she takes no notice.

CYMBELINE: The exile of Posthumus is too new;
She has not yet forgot him. Some more time
Must wear the print of his remembrance out,
And then she's yours.

QUEEN: You're indebted to the king,
Who lets go by no vantages that may
Prefer you to his daughter.

She picks up the boombox.

Frame yourself
To orderly solicits.

She throws the boombox at CLOTEN who catches it.

Make denials
Increase your services; so seem as if
You were inspired to do those duties which
You tender to her; that you in all obey her,
Save when command to your dismission tends,
And then feign a lack of understanding.

MESSENGER comes in.

MESSENGER: The ambassador from Rome. Caius Lucius.

CYMBELINE:	A worthy fellow,
	Albeit he comes on angry purpose now.
	But that's no fault of his. We must receive him
	According to the honour of his sender;

Everyone looks at each other.

And so extend our welcome. Our dear son,
When you have given good morning to Imogen,
Attend the queen and us.

He leaves and all follow except CLOTEN. Throughout his next speech we can see IMOGEN and HELEN and their responses.

CLOTEN: If she be up, I'll speak with her; if not,
Let her lie still and dream. *(Calls.)* IMOGEN!

No reply.

I know her woman is about her. What
If I do line her hand? It is gold
Which buys admittance; yeah, it does. I will make
Helen, her woman, lawyer to me; for
I yet not understand the case myself.

(Calls.) HELEN!

HELEN comes out.

CLOTEN: Your lady, is she ready?

HELEN: Ay.

CLOTEN: There is money for you if you sell me your good report.

IMOGEN barges through.

Good morrow, fairest. Sister, your sweet hand.

HELEN goes.

IMOGEN: Good morrow, sir. You lay out too much pains
And purchase only trouble; the thanks I give
Is telling you that I am poor of thanks
And scarce can spare them.

CLOTEN: Still, I swear I love you.

IMOGEN: So you swear still, your recompense is still
That I'll unfold equal discourtesy
To your best kindness!

She goes back into her room.

He follows her in.

CLOTEN: To leave you, in your madness, were my sin.
I will not.

IMOGEN: Fools cure not mad folks.

CLOTEN: Do you call me fool?

IMOGEN: As I am mad, I do:
If you would leave me, I'll no more be mad;
That cures us both. I am much sorry, sir,
You put me to forget a lady's manners,
By being so verbal! Please learn now, that I,
Who knows my heart, do here pronounce,
I care not for you – I hate you; which I had rather
You felt than make it my boast.

CLOTEN: You sin against
Obedience, which you owe your father. For
The contract you pretend with that base wretch,
One bred on cold dishes and scraps of the court,
It is no contract! You're curbed from that by
The consequence of the crown, and must not soil
The precious note of it with a base slave.

IMOGEN: He never can meet more mischance than come
To be so named by you. His meanest garment,
That ever has but touched his body, is dearer
In my respect than all the hairs above you.

IMOGEN grabs CLOTEN's hair and pulls his head down viciously.

He roars in pain and PISANIA comes rushing in. She pulls IMOGEN away.

How now, Pisania?

CLOTEN: His 'meanest garment'?

IMOGEN suddenly feels her wrist – looking around frantically.

IMOGEN: To Helen my woman bring her instantly –

CLOTEN: 'His garment!'

IMOGEN: I am haunted by a fool.

She goes for him but again is pulled back by PISANIA.

	Frighted, and angered worse. Go bid my woman
	Search for a jewel that too casually
	Has left my arm. It was my husband's. I think
	I saw it this morning. Confident I am,
	Last night it was on my arm; I kiss'd it!

PISANIA: It won't be lost.

IMOGEN: I hope not. Go and search.

PISANIA leaves.

CLOTEN: 'His meanest garment!'

IMOGEN: Ay, I said so, sir!
If you will make it an action,

She shoves him.

                     call witness to it.

CLOTEN: I will inform your father.

IMOGEN: Your mother too.
She's my good friend, and will conceive, I hope,
Only the worst of me. So, I leave you,
To the worst of discontent.

She pushes him out.

CLOTEN: I'll be revenged. 'His meanest garment!' Well.

SCENE TWELVE

Rome.

PHILARIA's house

PHILARIA and POSTHUMUS both stand expectantly.

PHILARIA lights a cigarette.

POSTHUMUS: Fear it not: I would I were so sure
To win the king as I am bold her honour
Will remain hers.

PHILARIA: What means do you make to him?

POSTHUMUS: Not any, but abide the change of time,
Quake in the present winter's state and wish
That warmer days would come!

GIACOMO appears.

See! Giacomo!

GIACOMO approaches. He gives nothing away.

PHILARIA: Giacomo!

POSTHUMUS: I hope the briefness of her answer made
The speediness of your return.

GIACOMO: Your lady
Is one of the fairest that I have looked upon.

POSTHUMUS: And therewithal the best!

GIACOMO: Letters for you.

POSTHUMUS: Their tenor good, I trust.

GIACOMO: It's very like.

PHILARIA: Was Caius Lucius in the Britain court
When you were there?

GIACOMO: He was expected then,
But not arrived.

POSTHUMUS has scanned his letter.

POSTHUMUS: All is well yet.
Sparkles this stone as it was wont or is it now
Too dull for your good wearing?

GIACOMO: If I have lost it,
Then I have lost the worth of it in gold.
I'll make a journey twice as far, to enjoy
A second night of such sweet shortness which
Was mine in Britain, for the ring is won.

POSTHUMUS: The stone's too hard to come by.

GIACOMO: Not a whit,
Your lady being so easy.

POSTHUMUS: Make not, now,
Your loss your sport. I hope you know that we
Must not continue friends.

GIACOMO: Had I not brought
The knowledge of your mistress home, I grant
We were to dispute further; but I now

> Profess myself the winner of her honour,
> Together with your ring; and not the wronger
> Of her or you, having proceeded but
> By both your wills.

POSTHUMUS: If you can make it apparent
> That you have tasted her in bed, my hand
> And ring is yours; if not –

GIACOMO: My circumstances,
> Being so near the truth as I will make them,
> Must induce you to believe.

POSTHUMUS: Proceed.

GIACOMO: Her bed –
> Where, I confess, I slept not, but profess
> Had that worth not sleeping for – it was dressed
> With tapestry of silk and silver –

POSTHUMUS: This is true;
> And this you might have heard of here, by me,
> Or by some other.

GIACOMO: More particulars
> Must justify my knowledge.

POSTHUMUS: So they must,
> Or do your honour injury.

GIACOMO: The window
> Is south the chamber –

POSTHUMUS: The description
> Of what is in her chamber nothing proves
> The wager you have laid.

GIACOMO: Then, if you can,
> Be pale: I beg but leave to air this jewel.

He shows the bracelet.

>   See!

He hides it.

> And now it's hid again. It must be married
> To that your diamond; I'll keep them.

POSTHUMUS: God!

Once more let me behold it: is it that
Which I left with her?

GIACOMO: She stripped it from her arm. I see her yet;
Her pretty action. She gave it me, and said
She prized it once.

POSTHUMUS: Maybe she plucked it off
To send it me.

GIACOMO: She writes so to you, does she?

POSTHUMUS scans the letters.

POSTHUMUS: No, no, no! It's true. Here, take this too.

He gives the ring to GIACOMO.

Kills me to look on it. Let there be no honour
Where there is beauty; truth, where semblance; love,
Where there's another man.

PHILARIA: Have patience, man,
And take your ring again; it's not yet won.
It's probable she lost the bracelet; or
Who knows if one of her women, being corrupted,
Hath stolen it from her?

POSTHUMUS: Very true;
And so, I hope, he came by it. Back my ring.

He takes the ring again.

Render to me some corporal sign about her,
More evident than that; for that was stolen.

GIACOMO: I swear, I had it from her arm.

POSTHUMUS: Listen, he swears, he swears it's true. Nay,
Keep the ring, I'm sure she would not lose it.
No, he has enjoyed her. There, take the ring –

He gives it to GIACOMO.

She has bought the name of whore and dearly.

PHILARIA: This is not strong enough to be believed
Of one persuaded well of –

POSTHUMUS: Never talk on it;
She has been colted by him.

GIACOMO: If you seek
For further satisfying, under her breast –
Worthy the pressing – lies a mole, right proud
Of that most delicate lodging. By my life,
I kissed it; and it gave me present hunger
To feed again, though full. You do remember
This stain upon her?

POSTHUMUS: Ay, and it confirms
Another stain, as big as hell can hold.

GIACOMO: Will you hear more?

POSTHUMUS: That I had her here, to tear her limb from limb!
I will go there and do it, in the court before
Her father. I'll do something.

                    He goes off.

PHILARIA: You have won:
Let's follow him, and pervert the present wrath
He has against himself.

GIACOMO: With all my heart.

SCENE THIRTEEN

CYMBELINE's warehouse.

Music.

CYMBELINE and QUEEN enter – followed by CLOTEN.

QUEEN looks fucked. She slightly wobbles off course – CLOTEN pulls her back.

CAIUS LUCIUS enters with other Romans.

The two groups face each other.

The music stops.

CYMBELINE: Now say, what would Augustus Caesar with us?

CAIUS: When Julius Caesar was in this Britain
And conquered it, Cassibelan, your uncle
Famous in Caesar's praises, and no more
Than in his feats deserving it – for him
And his succession granted Rome a tribute,

Yearly a weight in gold, which by you lately
Is left untendered.

QUEEN: And, to kill your wonder,
Shall be so ever.

CLOTEN: Come, there's no more tribute to be paid: our kingdom
is stronger than it was at that time!

CYMBELINE: Son, let your mother end.

CLOTEN: Why should we pay tribute? If Caesar can hide the sun
from us with a blanket, or put the moon in his pocket,
we will pay him tribute for light; else, no more tribute!

QUEEN: You must know,
Till the injurious Romans did extort
This tribute from us, we were free. Caesar's ambition,
Which swelled so much that it did almost stretch
The sides o' the world, against all reason here
Did force his will on us; which to shake off
Becomes a warlike people, whom we reckon
Ourselves to be.

CYMBELINE: We do.

He waits until QUEEN has settled down. Then continues.

                     And say so to Caesar –
Though Rome be therefore angry.

Pause.

CAIUS: I am sorry, Cymbeline,
Receive it from me, then: war and confusion
In Caesar's name pronounce I against you. Look
For fury not to be resisted. So, sir.

CYMBELINE: I know your master's pleasure and he mine.

Music.

They exit.

SCENE FOURTEEN

PISANIA is outside IMOGEN's room with a letter.

PISANIA: How? Of adultery? Why write you not
              What monster's her accuser? Posthumus,
              What false Roman, what strange infection is

              Fallen into your ear? Disloyal? No.
              She's punished for her truth, and undergoes,
              More goddess-like than wife-like, such assaults
              As would steal most virtue. Posthumus,
              Your mind to her is now as low as were
              Your fortunes. How? That I should murder her?
              Upon the love and truth and vows which I
              Have made to your command? I, her? Her blood?
              If it be so to do good service, never
              Let me be counted serviceable. How look I,
              That I should seem to lack humanity
              So much as this fact comes to?

              (*Reading.*)   'Do it: the letter
              That I have sent her, by her own command
              Shall give you opportunity.' You damned paper!
              Black as the ink that's on you!

              IMOGEN comes to her door.

IMOGEN: Pisania?

PISANIA: Here is a letter from –

              IMOGEN snatches the letter.

IMOGEN: Who? Posthumus!
              Learned indeed were that astronomer
              That knew the stars as I his characters –
              He'd lay the future open. Oh good God,
              Let what is here contained relish of love,
              Of my love's health, of his content – yet not
              That we two are apart; let that grieve him!

              She reads.

              'No matter how cruel Justice, and your father's wrath
              have been to me – you, the dearest of creatures, could
              renew me with your eyes. Take notice that I am at

Milford-Haven'.

He's at Milford-Haven!

Reads.

'What your own love will out of this advise you, follow.
So he wishes you all happiness, that remains loyal to his
vow, and yours, increasing in love,

                                        Posthumus.'

He is at Milford-Haven: read, and tell me
How far it is to there. Then, Pisania,
Who longs, like me, to see your friend; who longs, –
No that's not right – no not like me – you long,
But in a fainter kind – O, not like me;
For mine's beyond beyond. Say, how far it is
To this same blessed Milford. But first of all,
How we may steal from here? And how the gap,
That we shall make in time, from our leaving here
'Til our return, to excuse? But first, how from here?

PISANIA: Imogen, you'd best consider.

IMOGEN: I see before me, girl. For here, and here,
And what's behind, they have a fog in them,
That I cannot look through. No more to say,
Accessible is none but Milford way.

SCENE FIFTEEN

Milford.

A greenhouse full of cannabis plants.

BELARIUS, GUIDERIUS and ARVIRAGUS tend them.

ARVIRAGUS is deaf. He signs.

BELARIUS takes their tools away from them.

He gives a signal and they train – they do vigorous exercises – they play fight and they wrestle.

GUIDERIUS just begins to best ARVIRAGUS when BELARIUS steps in and with a couple of expert moves he pins both boys to the floor.

He gives them their tools back.

GUIDERIUS goes off and brings a large chunk of dead animal. BELARIUS wears a butcher's pinny and begins to cut into the meat.

BELARIUS:	This life is Richer than serving for worthless reward.
	GUIDERIUS groans.
ARVIRAGUS:	*(Signs.)* For fuck's sake!
	BELARIUS cuts and chops the meat.
BELARIUS:	If you'd known the city's money lenders And felt them knowingly; the art of the court, As hard to leave as keep; whose top to climb Is certain falling, or so slippery that The fear's as bad as falling; the toil of the war, A pain that only seems to seek out danger In the name of fame and honour; which dies in the search, And often has a slanderous epitaph As record of fair act! No life to ours.
GUIDERIUS:	*(Signs and speaks.)* Out of your proof you speak! Perhaps this life be best – If quiet life be best; sweeter to you That have a sharper known; well corresponding With your stiff age: but unto us it is A cell of ignorance.

ARVIRAGUS: *(Signs.)* What should we speak of
When we are old as you?

GUIDERIUS: We have seen nothing!

BELARIUS throws down his knife. He rips off his apron and top.
His body is covered in scars. He looks like he has been butchered.

BELARIUS: This story
The world may read in me. My body's marked
With Roman cuts, and my report was once
First with the best of note. Cymbeline loved me,
And when a soldier was the theme, my name
Was not far off. Then was I as a tree
Whose boughs did bend with fruit: but in one night,
A storm or robbery, call it what you will,
Shook me down and left me bare to weather.

GUIDERIUS: Uncertain favour!

BELARIUS: My fault being nothing – as I've told you often –
But that two villains, whose false oaths prevailed
Before my perfect honour, swore to Cymbeline
I was confederate with the Romans: so
Followed my banishment, and this twenty years
This place and these estates have been my world.

ARVIRAGUS: *(Signs.)* I'm sorry, father.

BELARIUS: *(Signs.)* Our valour is to chase what flies.

(Speaks.) Now for our sport!

Music.

He is hooking them up on wires to fly. They can climb at extraordinary
speed.

Your legs are young; I'll tread these flats. Consider,
When you above perceive me like a crow,
That it is place which lessens and sets off;
And you may then revolve what tales I have told you
Of courts, of princes, of the tricks in war!

He watches them climbing – leaping through the air.

He turns to us:

How hard it is to hide the sparks of nature!
These boys know little they are sons to the king;
Nor Cymbeline dreams that they are alive.
They think they are mine; and though trained up this meanly
Their thoughts do hit the roofs of palaces!

He points to GUIDERIUS.

This Polydore,
First son of Cymbeline and Britain, who
The king his father called Guiderius – God –
When on my three-legged stool I sit and tell
The warlike feats I have done, his spirits fly out
Into my story: say 'My enemy fell so,
And I set my foot on his neck' even then
The princely blood flows in his cheek, he sweats,
Strains his young nerves and puts himself in posture
That acts my words.

BELARIUS shows us. Miming the felling of some enemy and then viciously standing on his neck. He the points to ARVIRAGUS.

                  The younger brother, Cadwal,
Once Arviragus, in as like a figure,
Strikes life into my speech –

BELARIUS signs a short story of violence

                        – and shows much more
His own conceiving.

BELARIUS signs the same thing but with much more colour and violence.

O, Cymbeline, heaven and my conscience knows
You did unjustly banish me. Whereon,
At five and three years old, I stole these babes;
As you robbed me of my honour and my lands.
Myself, Belarius, that am Morgan called,
They take for natural father.

The boys land and the music stops.

                        The game is up.

SCENE SIXTEEN

Enter PISANIA and IMOGEN.

IMOGEN: You said to me, the place was near at hand!
Where is Posthumus? What is in your mind,
That makes you stare like that? What's the matter?

PISANIA offers the letter.

Why tender you that paper to me, with
A look untender? If it be summer news,
Smile at it now, if winterly, you need
But keep that countenance still.

PISANIA's expression doesn't change.

IMOGEN takes the letter.

My husband's hand.
Speak, girl! Your tongue
May take off some extremity, which to read
Would be even mortal to me.

PISANIA: Please read –
And you shall find me, wretched girl, a thing
The most disdained of fortune.

IMOGEN reads.

IMOGEN: 'Pisania, Imogen has played the whore in my bed; the
proof of this lies bleeding in me. Proof as strong as my
grief, and as certain as I expect my revenge. That part
you, Pisania, must act for me, if your faith be not tainted
with the breach of hers. Let your own hands take away
her life: I shall give you opportunity at Milford-Haven
– she has my letter for the purpose – where, if you fear
to strike and to make me certain it is done, you are an
accessory to her dishonour and to me disloyal.'

PISANIA: *(Aside.)* What shall I need to draw my blade? The paper
Has cut her throat already. No, it's slander!

IMOGEN: False to his bed! What is it to be false?
To lie in watch there and to think on him?
To break sleep with a fearful dream of him
And cry myself awake? That's false to his bed, is it?

PISANIA: Imogen.

IMOGEN: I false? Your conscience witness. Giacomo,
You did accuse him of incontinency,
And then looked like a villain; now I think
Your favour's good enough. Some jay of Rome
Whose mother was her painting, has betrayed him.
Poor I am stale, a garment out of fashion,

She starts to pull violently at her clothes.

I must be ripped – to pieces with me – O,
Men's vows are women's traitors! All good-seeming,
By your betrayal husband, shall be thought
Put on for villainy; a bait for ladies.

PISANIA: Imogen, hear me.

IMOGEN: Come, woman, you should
Do your master's bidding. When you see him,
A little witness my obedience. Look,
I draw the blade myself: take it, and hit
The innocent mansion of my love, my heart.
Fear not; it's empty of all things but grief.
Your master is not there, who was indeed
The riches of it. Do his bidding, strike.

PISANIA: You shall not damn my hand.

IMOGEN: Why, I must die;
And if I do not by your hand, you are
No servant of your master's. Here's my heart.
Something's afore it. Wait, wait!

She has letters stuffed in the front of her bra.

                             What is here?
The scriptures of the loyal Posthumus,
All turned to heresy? Away, away.

She throws them away.

I grieve myself to think, that when he's full
On her he feeds on now, how his memory
Will then be panged by me. Please, girl; dispatch.
The lamb begs the butcher! Where's your knife?

	You are too slow to do your friend's bidding,
	When I desire it too.
PISANIA:	Since I received command to do this business
	I have not slept one wink.
IMOGEN:	Do it, and to bed then.
PISANIA:	I'll wake mine eye-balls blind first.
IMOGEN:	Why then, did
	You undertake it? Why have you abused
	So many miles with a pretence? This place,
	My action and your own?
PISANIA:	But to win time
	To lose so bad employment; in the which
	I have considered of a course. Imogen,
	Hear me with patience.
IMOGEN:	Talk your tongue weary; speak.
	I have heard I am a whore; and mine ear
	Can take no greater wound. Speak.
PISANIA:	It cannot be
	But that Posthumus is abused,
	Some villain, ay, and singular in his art.
	Has done you both this cursed injury.
IMOGEN:	Some Roman prostitute.
PISANIA:	No! On my life.
	I'll give but notice you are dead, and send him
	Some bloody sign of it, for it's commanded
	I should do so. You shall be missed at court,
	And that will well confirm it.
IMOGEN:	Pisania,
	What shall I do the while? Where bide? How live?
	Or in my life what comfort, when I am
	Dead to my husband?
PISANIA:	If you'll back to the court –
IMOGEN:	No court, no father; nor no more ado
	With that harsh, empty, simple nothing,
	That Cloten, whose love-suit has been to me
	As fearful as a siege.

PISANIA: If not at court,
Then not in Britain must you bide.

IMOGEN: Where then?
Has Britain all the sun that shines? Day, night,
They are not just in Britain!

PISANIA: I'm most glad
You think of other place. The ambassador,
Caius the Roman, comes to Milford-Haven,
On his way to Rome. Offer your service.
Then you could tread a course haply near the
Residence of Posthumus; so near at least
That though his actions were not visible, yet
Report should render him hourly to your ear
As truly as he moves.

IMOGEN: For such means, through peril I'd adventure.

PISANIA: Well, then, here's the point:
You must forget to be a woman.

A pause.

IMOGEN: I see into your end, and am almost
A man already.

PISANIA: First make yourself but like one.
Fore-thinking this, I have already fit;
It's in my bag.

She throws a bag at IMOGEN's *feet.* IMOGEN *takes out some men's clothes.*

                        'Fore noble Lucius
Present yourself, desire his service, tell him
That is where you're happy. For means abroad,
You have me, rich; and I will never fail
In supplying.

IMOGEN *hugs her.*

IMOGEN: You are all the comfort
That God could feed me with.

IMOGEN *picks up the men's clothes.*

	This attempt
	I am soldier to, and will abide it with
	A prince's courage.

PISANIA: Let's take a short farewell,
Or, being missed, I'll be suspected of
Your carriage from the court. My dear Imogen,
Here is a box; I had it from the queen:
What's in it is precious; if you are sick,
A dram of this will drive away distemper.
Now, may God direct you!

PISANIA heads back the way they came.

IMOGEN calls after her.

IMOGEN: Amen. And thank you.

SCENE SEVENTEEN

At CYMBELINE's warehouse.

We see CAIUS LUCIUS and some Romans leaving.

They are observed by CYMBELINE, QUEEN, CLOTEN and CORNELIUS.

QUEEN is wired.

QUEEN: He goes hence frowning: but it honours us
That we have given him cause.

CLOTEN: It's all the better;
Your valiant Britons have their wishes in it.

CYMBELINE: Lucius has wrote already to Caesar
How it goes here. So be in readiness.
His powers will soon be drawn to head, and move
For war with Britain.

QUEEN: It's not sleepy business,
But must be looked to speedily and strongly.

CYMBELINE: Our expectation that it would be so
Has made us forward. But, my gentle queen,
Where is our daughter? She has not appeared
Before the Roman, nor to us has tendered
The duty of the day. She looks us like

A thing more made of malice than of duty.
We have noted it. Call her before us; for
We have been too slight in sufferance.

CARVILIUS goes off to get her.

QUEEN: Cymbeline,
Since the exile of Posthumus, most retired
Has her life been. The cure for this is time.
Avoid sharp speeches to her. She's a lady
So tender of rebukes that words are strokes
And strokes death to her.

CARVILIUS comes back.

CYMBELINE: Where is she, now? How
Can her contempt be answered?

CARVILIUS: Her chambers are all locked; and there's no answer
That will be given to the loudest noise we make.

QUEEN: My lord, when last I went to visit her,
She asked me to excuse her hiding there,
Whereby constrained by her unhappiness,
She should her duty leave unpaid to you.
She wished me to make this known.

CYMBELINE: Her doors locked?
Not seen of late? Please heaven, that which I fear
Prove false.

He leaves and is followed by CARVILIUS and CORNELIUS.

QUEEN: Son, I say, follow the king.

CLOTEN: That girl of hers, Pisania, I've not seen these two days.

QUEEN: Go, look after.

CLOTEN leaves.

QUEEN takes a coke bullet from inside her clothes. She twists it, then snorts.

Pisania, you that stands so for Posthumus!

She smashes something.

She turns to us.

She has a drug of mine. I pray her absence
Is caused by swallowing that, for she believes

It's a thing most precious. But Imogen,
Where is she gone? Perhaps, despair has seized her,
Or, winged with fervour of her love, she's flown
To her desired Posthumus. Gone she is
To death or to dishonour; and my end
Can make good use of either. She being down,
I have the placing of the British crown.

CLOTEN comes back in.

How now, my son?

CLOTEN: It's certain she is fled.
Go in and cheer the king: he rages; none
Dare come about him.

QUEEN: *(Aside.)*   All the better. May
This night deprive him of the coming day!

She reaches out to touch her son. He ignores her completely.

She leaves.

CLOTEN: Imogen: I love and hate her. For she
Has all parts more exquisite than every one,
Outsells them all – I love her therefore; but
Disdaining me and throwing favours on
The low Posthumus slanders so her judgment
That what's else rare is choked; and in that point
I will conclude to hate her. No, indeed,
To be revenged upon her.

PISANIA enters.

Who is here? What are you scheming, woman?
Where is Imogen? In a word; or else!

PISANIA: When was she missed?

CLOTEN: I'll have this secret from your heart, or rip
your heart to find it. Is she with Posthumus?

PISANIA: How can she be with him? He is in Rome.

CLOTEN takes out a knife.

CLOTEN: Speak, or your silence is your death.

PISANIA: Then, sir
This paper is the history of my knowledge
Touching her flight.

PISANIA presents a letter.

CLOTEN: Let's see it. I'll pursue her
Even to Augustus' throne.

Lights change. Sound stops. PISANIA moves away.

PISANIA: *(Aside.)*   It was this or die.
She's far enough; and what he learns by this
May prove his travel, but not her danger.

I'll write Posthumus she's dead. Imogen,
Safe may you wander, safe return again!

Lights change. Sound re-establishes. PISANIA returns to previous position.

CLOTEN: Pisania, is this letter true?

PISANIA: Yes.

CLOTEN: It is Posthumus' hand. I know it. If you would not be
a villain, but do me true service – that is; whatever
villainy I bid you do, to perform it truly – you should
neither want for means or preferment. Will you serve
me?

PISANIA: I will.

CLOTEN: Give me your hand.

CLOTEN counts out a large amount of notes.

Have you any of Posthumus' garments in your
possession?

PISANIA: I have the same he wore when he took leave of Imogen.

CLOTEN: The first service you do me, fetch that suit here. Go!

PISANIA leaves.

CLOTEN looks back to the letter.

CLOTEN: 'Meet you at Milford-Haven'. There, Posthumus, will
I kill you. I would these clothes were come. Imogen
said – the bitterness of it I now belch from my heart –
that she held his very garment in more respect than my

person. On his dead body will I ravish her; and when
my lust has dined – which, as I say, to vex her I will
execute in his clothes that she so praised – to the court
I'll knock her back, foot her home again.

PISANIA comes in with POSTHUMUS' clothes.

Be those the garments?

PISANIA: Yes.

CLOTEN: How long is it since she went to Milford-Haven?

PISANIA: She can scarce be there yet.

CLOTEN: My revenge is now at Milford. Would I had wings to
follow it! Come, and be true.

They leave.

SCENE EIGHTEEN

IMOGEN comes on in boy's clothes.

IMOGEN: I see a man's life is a tedious one.
I have tired myself, and for two nights together
Have made the ground my bed. I should be sick,
But that my resolution helps me.
Two beggars told me
I could not miss my way: will poor folks lie,
That have afflictions on them, knowing it's
A punishment or trial? Yes; no wonder,
When rich ones scarce tell true. To lapse in fullness
Is sorer than to lie for need, and falsehood
Is worse in kings than beggars. Posthumus,
You are one o' the false ones. Now I think on you,
My hunger's gone –

She sees the greenhouse.

                          But what is this?
I were best not to call; I dare not call; yet famine,
Makes me valiant. Hello! Who is there?
Hello! Hi! No answer? Then I'll enter.

She goes in.

49

BELARIUS, GUIDERIUS and ARVIRAGUS come in from different directions.

GUIDERIUS pulls lots of different food packets from his top.

ARVIRAGUS pulls out just one packet.

BELARIUS: You, Polydore, are master of the feast!
Cadwal will play the cook. Come; our stomachs
Will make what's homely savoury!

BELARIUS sets off to the greenhouse.

GUIDERIUS: I am thoroughly weary.

ARVIRAGUS: *(Signs.)* I am weak with toil, yet strong in appetite.

BELARIUS: Stay; come not in.
But that it's eating our food, I should think
Here were an angel. Behold divineness
No elder than a boy!

IMOGEN comes out of the greenhouse.

IMOGEN: Please, harm me not:
Before I entered here, I called; and thought
To have bought what I have taken. Good truth,
I have stolen nought, nor would not.

She takes out some notes.

Here's money for my food.

GUIDERIUS: Money, youth?

ARVIRAGUS: *(Signed.)* All gold and silver rather turn to dirt!

He gives the thumbs up to BELARIUS, who nods his approval.

IMOGEN: I see you're angry:
Know, if you kill me for my fault, I should
Have died had I not made it.

BELARIUS: What's your name?

IMOGEN: Fidele.

BELARIUS: Think us no churls, nor measure our good minds
By this rude place we live in. Well encountered!
It's almost night. You shall have better food
'Fore you go, and are welcome to stay and eat it.

GUIDERIUS and ARVIRAGUS are staring in awe at IMOGEN.

	Boys, bid him welcome.
GUIDERIUS:	Were you a woman, youth, I should woo hard!
ARVIRAGUS:	*(Signs and BELARIUS interprates.)* To console himself, For your being a man he'll love you as his brother. And such a welcome as he'd give to him After long absence, such is yours. Most welcome!

They all enjoy hugging IMOGEN.

| IMOGEN: | Amongst friends, if brothers. |

Lights change. Sound stops. IMOGEN moves away. She walks around GUIDERIUS and ARVIRAGUS.

| IMOGEN: | Great men, could not out-peer these two. |

She imitates their stance.

Forgive me, God,
I'd change my sex to be companion with them,
Posthumus now being false.

Lights change. Sound re-establishes. IMOGEN returns to previous position.

BELARIUS:	Boys, we'll go eat our food. Fair youth, come in. Discourse is heavy, fasting. When we have supped, We'll mannerly demand of you your story, So far as you will speak it.
GUIDERIUS:	Please, draw near.
ARVIRAGUS:	*(Signs.)* Please, draw near.
IMOGEN:	Thank you.

They all go into the greenhouse.

SCENE NINETEEN

Rome.

CAIUS LUCIUS, GIACOMO, PHILARA, and others.

CAIUS hands PHILARIA some papers and she distributes them.

| GIACOMO: | Is Lucius general of the forces? |

PHILARIA: To undertake our war against the Britons,
Caesar creates Lucius pro-consul.
For this immediate action, he commends
His absolute authority.

She indicates the paper she has handed to him.

The words of your commission
Will tie you to the numbers and the time
Of our dispatch.

CAIUS gives her a signal and she follows him as he leaves.
GIACOMO is left alone.

GIACOMO: We will discharge our duty.

SCENE TWENTY

CLOTEN in POSTHUMUS' tracksuit.

CLOTEN: I am near to the place where they should meet, if
Pisania have mapped it truly. How fit his garments serve
me. Why should his wife, not fit too? I mean, the lines
of my body are as well drawn as his; no less young,
more strong, not beneath him in fortunes, above him
in birth, yet this imperceiverant thing loves him in my
despite. Posthumus, your head, which now is on your
shoulders, shall within this hour be off; your woman
enforced; your garments cut to pieces before her face.
And all this done, spurn her home to her father; who
may perhaps be a little angry for my so rough usage;
but my mother, having power of his testiness, shall turn
all into my commendations. Out, blade, and to a sore
purpose! Fortune, put them into my hand! This is the
very description of their meeting-place; and Pisania
dares not deceive me.

SCENE TWENTY-ONE

GUIDERIUS and ARVIRAGUS come out of the greenhouse.

GUIDERIUS: I could not stir him:
He said he was honest, but unfortunate.

ARVIRAGUS: *(Signs)* Such did he answer me: yet said, hereafter
I might know more.

IMOGEN comes out followed by BELARIUS.

BELARIUS: You are not well: remain here in our home.
We'll come to you after working.

ARVIRAGUS: *(Signed and interpreted by GUIDERIUS.)* Brother, stay here.
Are we not brothers?

IMOGEN: So man and man should be!
I am very sick.

GUIDERIUS: I'll abide with him.

IMOGEN: Stick to your course. I'm ill, but your being by me
Cannot amend me. Society is no comfort
To one not sociable. I'm not very sick,
Since I can reason of it.

GUIDERIUS: I love you. I have spoke it:
How much the quantity, the weight? As much
As I do love my father.

BELARIUS: What, how, how?

ARVIRAGUS: *(Signs. Interpreted by BELARIUS)* If it be sin to say so, I find I
Share my good brother's fault. I know not why
I love this youth; and I have heard you say,
Love's reason is without reason. A threat at door,
And a demand, 'who is it shall die?', I'd say,
'My father, not this youth.'

GUIDERIUS: Brother, farewell.

IMOGEN: I wish you sport.

BELARIUS, GUIDERIUS and ARVIRAGUS move away.

    (Aside.)   These are kind creatures.
I am sick still; heart-sick.

She sobs.

Pisania,

I'll now taste of your drug.

She takes it out and drinks.

She sings. It's sad and beautiful.

GUIDERIUS and ARVIRAGUS have crept back and are watching IMOGEN.

BELARIUS also returns and watches them watching her.

IMOGEN walks into the greenhouse, still singing.

BELARIUS: To the field, to the field!
This youth, however distressed, appears he has
Good ancestors.

ARVIRAGUS: *(Signs.)* He is beautiful.

GUIDERIUS: *(Signs and speaks.)*
Yes. And sings like an angel. And I do note
That grief and patience, rooted in him both,
Mingle their spurs together.

BEARIUS: Come, away!
Who's there?

CLOTEN has appeared.

CLOTEN: I cannot find those traitors. That villain
Has mocked me.

BELARIUS: 'Those traitors!'
Means he not us? I think I know him: It's
Cloten, the son of the queen. I fear some ambush.
I know it's he. We are held as outlaws. Go!

GUIDERIUS: He is but one. You and my brother search
What companies are near. Pray you, away,
Let me alone with him.

He reveals himself as the others head off.

CLOTEN: What are you?

They circle each other with their knives.

Give up, villain!

GUIDERIUS: To who? To you? Have not I
An arm as big as yours? A heart as big?

	Your words, I grant, are bigger, for I wear not My dagger in my mouth. Say what you are.
CLOTEN:	Know me not by my clothes?
GUIDERIUS:	No, nor your tailor, Who is your grandfather! He made those clothes, Which, as it seems, make you. You are some fool. I'm loath to beat you.
CLOTEN:	Hear my name, and tremble.
GUIDERIUS:	What's your name?
CLOTEN:	Cloten, you villain.
GUIDERIUS:	Cloten, you double villain, be your name, I cannot tremble at it. A spider Would move me sooner.
CLOTEN:	To your further fear, You shall know that I am son to the queen.
GUIDERIUS:	I am sorry for it; you're not seeming So worthy as your birth.
CLOTEN:	You're not afraid!
GUIDERIUS:	Those that I reverence, those I fear, the wise: At fools I laugh, not fear them.

They fight. The fight is a vicious knife fight.

People move in around it.

A bag is filled with blood.

GUIDERIUS cuts off CLOTEN's head with his knife.

The bag of blood is handed to GUIDERIUS.

BELARIUS and ARVIRAGUS enter.

BELARIUS:	No companies abroad?
ARVIRAGUS:	*(Signs.)* None in the world: you did mistake him, sure.
BELARIUS:	I am absolute, it was very Cloten. But, see, your brother –
	GUIDERIUS appoaches with the bag of blood. It's CLOTEN's head.
GUIDERIUS:	This Cloten was a fool –
BELARIUS	What have you done?

GUIDERIUS   Yet I not doing this, the fool had borne
       My head as I do his.

BELARIUS: We are all undone.

GUIDERIUS: Why, worthy father, should we be so meek
       To let an arrogant piece of flesh threat us,
       Play judge and executioner all himself?
       What company discover you abroad?

BELARIUS: No single soul. But in all safe reason
       He must have some attendants. And perhaps
       It may be heard at court that such as we
       Live here, work here, are outlaws, and in time
       May make some stronger force; the which he hearing –
       As it is like him – might break out, and swear
       He'd fetch us in. Yet it is not probable
       To come alone. Then on good ground we fear,
       If we do fear this body has a tail
       More perilous than the head.

ARVIRAGUS: *(Signs.)* Howsoever, my brother has done well.

       He holds GUIDERIUS' shoulders.

GUIDERIUS: *(Signs and speaks.)* With his own blade,
       Which he did wave against my throat, I have taken
       His head from him. I'll throw it in the creek.
       And tell the fishes he's the queen's son, Cloten!
       That's all I reck.

       He leaves with the head.

BELARIUS: I fear it'll be revenged.

ARVIRAGUS: *(Signs.)*
       Would I had done't so the revenge alone pursued me!
       I would revenges, that possible strength might meet,
       And put us to our answer.

BELARIUS: Well, it's done.
       You and Fidele play the cooks. I'll stay
       Till hasty Polydore return, and bring him
       To dinner presently.

ARVIRAGUS: *(Signs.)*   Poor sick Fidele!
       I'll willingly to him.

He heads into the greenhouse.

BELARIUS: Yet still it's strange
What Cloten's being here to us portends,
Or what his death will bring us.

GUIDERIUS comes back.

GUIDERIUS: Where's my brother?
I have sent Cloten's fat head down the stream.

ARVIRAGUS comes out of the greenhouse carrying IMOGEN.

GUIDERIUS runs to them. Touches IMOGENs face.

GUIDERIUS: O sweetest, fairest lily!
My brother wears you not the one half so well
As when you grew yourself.

He helps his brother lower IMOGEN to the ground.

BELARIUS: You blessed thing!
God knows what man you might have made; I know
You died, a most rare boy, of melancholy.
(Signs and speaks.) How found you him?

ARVIRAGUS: *(Signs.)* Stark, as you see
Thus smiling, as some fly had tickled slumber,
Not as death's dart, being laughed at; his right cheek
Reposing on a cushion.

GUIDERIUS: Where?

ARVIRAGUS: *(Signs.)* O' the floor;
His arms thus leagued: I thought he slept.

GUIDERIUS: Yes – it's like he sleeps.

GUIDERIUS strokes IMOGEN's face and hair.

If he be gone, we'll make his grave a bed!

Music.

The three of them position IMOGEN.

They bring flowers and cannabis leaves from the greenhouse and stand around the grave.

ARVIRAGUS: *(Signs.)* And let us, sing him to the ground,

BELARIUS: *(Signs and speaks.)* I cannot sing: I'll weep notes of sorrow

ARVIRAGUS: *(Signs.)* Well speak it, then.

BELARIUS: I'll word it with you. So begin.

ARVIRAGUS signs the following. BELARIUS watches his hands intently and interprets.

ARVIRAGUS: With fairest flowers,
Whilst summer lasts and I live here, Fidele,
I'll sweeten your sad grave. You shall not lack
The flower that's like your face, pale primrose, nor
The azured harebell, like your veins, no, nor
The leaf of eglantine, whom not to slander,
Outsweetens not your breath. I'll bring all this
Yes, and furred moss besides, when flowers are none,
To winter-ground your bed.

GUIDERIUS touches IMOGEN's face.

GUIDERIUS: Fear no more the heat o' the sun,
Nor the furious winter's rages.

The music disappears and they stand in silence.

BELARIUS: Great griefs, I see, cure the less; for Cloten
Is quite forgot.

He heads over to CLOTEN's headless body.

He was a queen's son, boys;
And though you took his life, as being our foe,
Yet bury him as a prince.

GUIDERIUS: Fetch him here.
One body is as good as another,
When neither are alive.

BELARIUS has dragged CLOTEN's body to beside IMOGEN's grave.

Come, lay him down.

BELARIUS takes some of the petals around and scatters them over CLOTEN's body.

BELARIUS: Here's a few flowers; strewings fit for graves.
The ground that gave them first has them again:
Their pleasures here are past, so is their pain.

The three of them leave.

All is still and silent for some time.

IMOGEN wakes up.

IMOGEN   Yes, please to Milford – which is the way?
           You're jokin'! How far? Is it six mile's still?
           Nah, I've gone all night. I'll lie down and sleep.

           She makes contact with CLOTEN's body.

           She jolts upwards.

           But, soft! no bedfellow!

           She sees the body.

                             O, God what a sight!
           These flowers are like the pleasures of the world;
           This bloody man, the horrors. I hope I dream:
           For so I thought I was a home-keeper,
           And cook to honest creatures, but it's not so;
           Was but a bolt of nothing, shot at nothing,
           Which the brain makes of fumes. Our very eyes
           Are sometimes like our judgments, blind. Good faith,
           I tremble still with fear: but if there be
           Yet left in heaven as small a drop of pity
           As a wren's eye, feared God, a part of it.
           The dream's here still. Even when I wake, it is
           Without me, as within me; not imagined, felt.
           A headless man. The garments of Posthumus.
           I know the shape of his leg; this is his hand,
           His arm, his warrior brawn. But his godlike face –
           Murder in heaven! How? It's gone. Pisania,
           All my curses be darted on you! You,
           Conspiring with that lawless devil, Cloten,
           Have cut off Posthumus. To write and read
           Be henceforth treacherous! Damned Pisania
           Has with her forged letters – damned Pisania –
           From this most bravest vessel of the world
           Struck the main-top! O, Posthumus, my love,
           Where is your head? Where's that? Ay me, where's that?
           Pisania might have killed you at the heart,
           And left this head on. How should this be? Pisania?
           It's she and Cloten: malice and greed in them
           Have laid this woe here. O, it's pregnant, pregnant!
           The drug she gave me, which she said was precious

And cordial to me, have I not found it
Murderous to the senses? That confirms it home.
This is Pisania's deed, and Cloten's. O, –
Give colour to my pale cheek with your blood,

She rubs her hands into his wounds.

That we the horrider may seem to those

She rubs the blood over her face and hair and clothes.

Which chance to find us. O, my love, my love.

She falls on the body.

Enter LUCIUS, GIACOMO, PHILARIA and other Romans.

CAIUS: This forwardness
Makes our hopes fair. Command our present numbers
Be mustered; bid the captains look to it.

Someone leaves.

What trunk is here without his top? A boy;
Is dead, or sleeping on him? Let's see his face.

PHILARIA turns IMOGEN.

PHILARIA: He's alive, Caius.

CAIUS: He'll then instruct us of this body. Young one,
Inform us of your fortunes. Who is this
You make your bloody pillow? Or who was he
That altered that good picture? How came it?
What are you?

IMOGEN: I am nothing: or if not,
Nothing to be were better. This was my friend,
A very valiant Briton and a good,
That here by runaways lies slain. Alas!
There are no more such friends: I may wander
From east to west, try many; and never
Find such another one.

CAIUS: Listen, good youth!
You move no less with your lamenting than
Your friend in bleeding. Say his name, good friend.

IMOGEN struggles.

IMOGEN: Richard.

CAIUS:	Richard?
IMOGEN:	Richards.
CAIUS:	Richard Richards?

IMOGEN nods.

IMOGEN:	Richard Richards. *(Aside.)* If I do lie and do
	No harm by it, though that God hears, I hope
	He'll pardon it.
CAIUS:	Your name?
IMOGEN:	Fidele.
PHILARIA:	Boy,
	You do approve yourself the very same:
	Your name well fits your faith, your faith your name.
CAIUS:	Will you take your chance with me? Go with me?
IMOGEN:	I'll follow, sir. But first, I must hide my friend
	From the flies.

CAIUS instructs his people.

CAIUS:	Come, lift him.
PHILARIA:	Boy, he is preferred
	By you to us, and he shall be interred
	As soldiers are.
CAIUS:	Be cheerful; wipe your eyes.
	Some falls are means the happier to arise.

SCENE TWENTY-TWO

CYMBELINE's warehouse.

The curtains close off an area. Within it we see QUEEN – she is half-dressed and wanders aimlessly.

She falls to her knees and sobs. She hits herself.

She stands and wanders.

She falls to her knees and sobs. She hits herself.

She is destroyed.

CYMBELINE:	Doctor, give me word how it is with her.

CORNELIUS: A fever with the absence of her son,
    A madness, of which her life's in danger.

CYMBELINE: Heaven,
    How deeply you at once do touch me! Imogen,
    The great part of my comfort, gone; my queen
    Lost to a desperate state, and in a time
    When fearful wars point at me; her son gone,
    So needful for this present. It strikes me, past
    The hope of comfort.

He waves the doctor away. The doctor goes inside the curtained area and leads QUEEN away.

PISANIA is brought before CYMBELINE.

          Now for you, woman,
    Who has to know of her departure yet
    Do seem so ignorant. We'll enforce it from you
    By a sharp torture.

The curtains are opened.

A chair is revealed. CARVILIUS and HELEN stand by it.

They suddenly go for PISANIA. They hold her over the chair. The pull up the back of her clothes revealing her naked back. One of them holds a blade to her back.

PISANIA: Sir, of your daughter,
    I nothing know where she remains, why gone,
    Nor when she purposes return.

CYMBELINE rushes over and throws her to the floor. He takes his own knife out and holds it to her throat.

CYMBELINE: Where is she?

HELEN: Cymbeline,
    The day Imogen was missed, she was here!
    I dare be bound she's true and shall perform
    All parts of her subjection loyally. For Cloten,
    We show all diligence in seeking him,
    And will, no doubt, be found.

CYMBELINE: The time is troublesome.
    We will let you slip; but our suspicion
    Remains.

CORNELIUS comes in.

CORNELIUS: The Romans are by Caesar sent.

CYMBELINE: Now for the counsel of my son and queen!
I am amazed with matter.

CARVILIUS: Your preparation can affront no less
Than that you hear of. Come more, for more you're ready.
The want is but to put those powers in motion
That long to move.

CYMBELINE: I thank you. Let's withdraw;
And meet the time as it seeks us. We fear not
What can from Italy annoy us; but
We grieve at matters here. Away!
All leave.

SCENE TWENTY-THREE

Music. A sense of a battle.

GUIDERIUS: The noise is round about us.

BELARIUS: Let us from it.

GUIDERIUS: What hope have we in hiding us? This way,
The Romans must for Britons slay us.

BELARIUS: Sons,
To the king's party there's no going. For
What we have done, the answer would be death
Drawn on with torture.

GUIDERIUS: This is, sir, a doubt
In such a time nothing becoming you,
Nor satisfying us.

ARVIRAGUS: *(Signs.)* It is not likely
That they will waste their time upon our note,
To know from where we came.

BELARIUS: I am known
Of many with Cymbeline; who, besides,
Has not deserved my service nor your loves.

GUIDERIUS: I and my brother are not known; yourself
So out of thought.

ARVIRAGUS: *(Signs.)* By this sun that shines,
I'll go there. What thing is it that I never
Did see man die, scarce ever looked on blood?
I am ashamed to have
The benefit of his blest beams, remaining
So long a poor unknown.

GUIDERIUS: By heaven, I'll go.
If you will bless me, sir, and give me leave,
I'll take the better care, but if you will not,
The hazard therefore due fall on me by
The hands of Romans!

ARVIRAGUS: *(Signs.)* So say I. Amen.

BELARIUS: No reason I, since of your lives you set
So slight a valuation, should reserve
My cracked one to more care. Have with you, boys!
If in these Briton wars you chance to die,
That is my bed too, lads, and there I'll lie.
Lead, lead.

They head towards the Britons.

SCENE TWENTY-FOUR

The Romans.

Drinking. Training. Handing out weapons.

POSTHUMUS looks at the audience. Looks at every man.

POSTHUMUS: You married ones,
If each of you should take this course, how many
Would murder wives much better than themselves
For wrying but a little? O, Pisania!
Every good servant does not all commands.
No bond, but to do just ones. God, if you
Had taken vengeance on my faults, I'd never
Had lived to have started all this; and you'd have saved

The noble Imogen to repent, and struck
Me, wretch, more worth your vengeance.

The Romans begin to move away to go and fight. IMOGEN is with them.

I'm brought here
Among the Roman soldiers, and to fight
Against Imogen's father. It's enough
That, Britain, I have killed your daughter; peace,
I'll give no wound to you. Therefore, good heaven,
Hear patiently my purpose: I'll disrobe me
Of these Roman weeds; and then I'll fight

He takes off his top.

Against the part I come with; so I'll die
For you, O, Imogen, even for whom my life
Is every breath a death. To this peril
Myself I'll dedicate. Let me make men know
More valour in me than my actions have shown.

Loud music. He puts on a mask.

SCENE TWENTY-FIVE.

A battle.

A curtained area has been filled with smoke.

The curtains open to reveal the Romans versus the Britons.

Many wear masks or scarves to cover their faces.

Many of the Britons are bare-chested.

A mad chaotic fight. It is hard to know who is on which side.

IMOGEN is in the centre of it. She avoids conflict not wanting to harm any Briton.

Blood is everywhere.

POSTHUMUS and GIACOMO end up in a skirmish. POSTHUMUS is about to kill GIACOMO – but leaves him.

GIACOMO: The heaviness and guilt within my bosom
Takes off my manhood. I have slandered a woman,
The daughter of this country, and its air
Revengingly enfeebles me.

CYMBELINE comes into focus fighting two Romans. GIACOMO joins with them and CYMBELINE is overpowered and captured.

IMOGEN watches in horror. She makes the mistake of pulling one Roman away. That Roman goes to kill her but is stopped by CAIUS LUCIUS.

BELARIUS, GUIDERIUS, ARVIRAGUS and POSTHUMUS appear.

GIACOMO: It's their fresh supplies.

BELARIUS, GUIDERIUS, ARVIRAGUS and POSTHUMUS attack the Romans and free CYMBELINE. BELARIUS turns to all Britons.

BELARIUS: Stand, stand! We have the advantage of the ground!

On instinct IMOGEN heads towards the Britons one of them hits her hard and she collapses – but CAIUS LUCIUS pulls her back.

CAIUS: Away, boy, from the fray, and save yourself;
For friends kill friends, and the disorder's such
As war were hoodwinked.

IMOGEN runs away.

Another mass skirmish; the Britons clearly have the upper hand.

They are fighting on top of a pile of dead bodies.

Everyone is covered in blood/paint.

CAIUS LUCIUS grabs GIACOMO.

CAIUS: Let's reinforce, or fly.

They move back and finally run off.

GUIDERIUS roars after them:

GUIDERIUS: Stand, stand, and fight!

The Britons give chase.

A sudden blackout.

Silence.

SCENE TWENTY-SIX

POSTHUMUS staggers in, exhausted, carrying his mask.

Bodies everywhere.

A dead Roman is at his feet.

POSTHUMUS: To-day how many would have given their honour
To have saved their carcass; took heel to do it,
And yet died still. I, in my too charmed life,
Could not find death where I did hear him groan,
Nor feel him where he struck. Well, I will find him.
And as he's shown his favour to the Britons:
No more a Briton.

He throws away his mask. He steals a sweatshirt from a Roman corpse.

                        I have resumed again
The part I came in. Fight I will no more,
But surrender to the meanest hand that shall
First touch my shoulder.

CARVILIUS, PISANIA and another BRITON arrive.

CARVILIUS: Lucius is taken.
It's thought the old man and his sons were angels.

PISANIA: There was a fourth gave the affront with them.

CARVILIUS: But none of 'em can be found. Stand! Who's there?

POSTHUMUS: A Roman.

PISANIA: A dog!

CARVILIUS: Lay your hands on him.

They overpower POSTHUMUS and bind his hands with cable ties. They put a hood over his head.

Bring him to Cymbeline.

SCENE TWENTY-SEVEN

POSTHUMUS is pushed to his knees beside other Roman prisoners. All on their knees, hoods over their heads and hands cable-tied behind their back.

CYMBELINE by a fire.

Stood apart are BELARIUS, GUIDERIUS and ARVIRAGUS.

CYMBELINE: Stand by my side, you three who God has made
    Preservers of my throne. Sad is my heart
    That the poor soldier whose naked breast
    Stepped before blades of proof, cannot be found.
    He shall be happy that can find him, if
    Our grace can make him so.

BELARIUS: I never saw
    Such noble fury.

CYMBELINE: No tidings of him?

PISANIA: No trace of him.

CYMBELINE: To my grief, I am
    The heir of his reward which I will add
    To you, knights of the battle. I create you
    Companions to our person and will fit you
    With dignities becoming your estates.

    CORNELIUS and HELEN come in. They are clean – not covered in blood.

    There's business in these faces. Why so sadly
    Greet you our victory?

CORNELIUS: Cymbeline,
    To sour your happiness, I must report
    The queen is dead.

    Silence.

CYMBELINE: Who worse than a physician
    Could this report come from?

    He signals and CORNELIUS is dragged onto a chair. His face smashed into a table. A torch is lit and held in front of CORNELIUS. CYMBELINE roars at him.

But I consider,
By medicine life should be prolonged, yet death
Will seize the doctor too.

CORNELIUS' face is smashed into the table again, this time by CYMBELINE. CYMBELINE walks away until he has calmed.

How ended she?

A light comes on somewhere in the stage and we see the image of QUEEN. She wears a man's vest and nothing else. She is pulling it. Distorting it's shape and her own.

CORNELIUS: With horror, madly dying, like her life,
Which, being cruel to the world, concluded
Most cruel to herself. What she confessed
I will report. This her woman was there.
She can stop me if I tell it false.

CYMBELINE: Say.

CORNELIUS: First, she confessed

QUEEN joins in here (see below).

                          she never loved you, only
Married your greatness, was wife to your place;
Abhorred your person.

QUEEN: I never loved him, only
Married his greatness, was wife to his place;
Abhorred his person.

CYMBELINE: She alone knew this;
Had she not spoke it dying, I would not
Believe her lips in opening it. Proceed.

CORNELIUS: Your daughter, whom she did pretend to love
Was as a scorpion to her sight; whose life,
But that her flight prevented it, she would have
Taken off by poison.

QUEEN: *(At the same time.)*   His daughter, who I did pretend to love
Was as a scorpion to my sight; whose life,
But that her flight prevented it, I would have
Taken off by poison.

CYMBELINE: Who is it can read a woman?

There is now only light on QUEEN. She smokes and at the same time injects into her arm.

QUEEN: I have
For him a mortal mineral; which, when he takes,
Will by the minute feed on life, and lingering
By inches waste him. In which time I plan,
By watching, weeping, tendance, kissing, to
Overcome him with my show, and in time,
When I have finished him with my craft, to work
My son into the adoption of the crown.

Lights come back up on CORNELIUS.

CORNELIUS: But, failing of her aim by Cloten's absence,
Grew shameless-desperate; opened, in despite
Of heaven and men, her purposes; repented
The evils she hatchd were not effected; so
Despairing died.

CYMBELINE goes to HELEN.

CYMBELINE: Heard you all this?

HELEN: I did.

CYMBELINE: Mine eyes
Were not in fault, for she was beautiful;
Mine ears, that heard her flattery; nor my heart,
That thought her like she seemed. O, Imogen
That it was folly in me you may say,
And your ill treatment proves it.

CAIUS LUCIUS, GIACOMO, IMOGEN and POSTHUMUS are brought down to CYMBELINE by CARVILIUS and HELEN.

CAIUS LUCIUS' hood is taken off.

Caius, you come not now for tribute.

CAIUS: Consider, now, the chance of war. The day
Was yours by accident. Had it gone with us,
We should not, when the blood was cool, have threatened
Our prisoners.

CYMBELINE nods and his people move in on CAIUS and string him up in the air by his wrists.

Everyone panics – lots of shouting and screaming.

>   If nothing but our lives
> May be called ransom, let it come. This death
> A Roman with a Roman's heart can suffer.
> Augustus Caesar lives! So think on it!

CYMBELINE takes off IMOGEN's hood.

BELARIUS: Is not this boy revived from death?

GUIDERIUS: The same dead thing alive.

BELARIUS: Let's see further.

CAIUS: This one thing only I will ask: That boy,
Is a Briton born; let him be ransomed.
A boy so kind, duteous, diligent;
When his virtue join with my request, you
Cannot deny! He has done no Briton harm.
Though he have served a Roman, spare him, if,
You spare no blood beside.

CYMBELINE: I have surely seen him:
His favour is familiar to me. Boy,
You have looked yourself into my grace,
And are mine own. I know not why I say,
'Live, boy'.

He cuts her free.

              Thank not Caius Lucius. Live.
And ask of Cymbeline what you will. I'll
Give it.

IMOGEN: I humbly thank you, Cymbeline.

Knelt next to GIACOMO, IMOGEN notices his hands.

CAIUS: I do not bid you beg my life, good lad;
And yet I know you will.

IMOGEN: No, no; sorry.
There's other work in hand: I see a thing
Bitter to me as death: your life, good Caius,
Must shuffle for itself.

CAIUS: The boy disdains me.
Why stands he so perplexed?

CYMBELINE: What is it, boy?

Noticing that IMOGEN stares at GIACOMO. CYMBELINE takes off his hood.

Know him you look on? Speak. Would have him live?
Is he your kin? Your friend?

IMOGEN: He is a Roman.
No more kin to me than I am to you.

CYMBELINE: Why d'you eye him so?

IMOGEN: I'll tell you in
Private, if you please to give me hearing.

CYMBELINE: And lend my best attention.

They begin to move away.

                                   What's your name?

IMOGEN: Fidele.

They whisper together.

PISANIA: *(Aside.)* It's Imogen.
Since she is living, let the time run on
To good or bad.

CYMBELINE and IMOGEN return.

CYMBELINE: Come and stand by my side;
Make your demand aloud.

He cuts GIACOMO free.

                                   You, stand you up.
Give answer to this boy and do it freely.

IMOGEN: My wish is that this gentleman may tell
Of whom he had this ring.

GIACOMO: What's that to you?

CYMBELINE: That diamond! Say now how came it yours? Or
Bitter torture shall make you speak to him.

GIACOMO: That to be spoke will torture you.

CYMBELINE: How me?

GIACOMO: Upon a time – unhappy was the clock
That struck the hour – in Rome, good Posthumus,
Hearing us praise women of our country,
Praised Imogen, your daughter – give me leave, I faint.

CYMBELINE grabs him.

CYMBELINE: My daughter! What of her?

IMOGEN pulls GIACOMO from CYMBELINE and shakes him.

IMOGEN: Strive, man, and speak.

CARVILIUS grabs GIACOMO and smashes his face into the table and a torch is held close to his face.

GIACOMO: Your daughter's faithfulness – there it begins.
Posthumus spoke of her, and I, wretch, was
Dismissive of his praise; and wagered with him
(My money against this stone) that I could,
Take his place in her bed and win this ring
By hers and mine adultery. He, true soul,
No lesser of her honour confident
Than I did truly find her, stakes this ring.
I came away to Britain: well may you,
Remember me at court; where I was quenched
By your good daughter, of hope, not longing.
I returned to Rome with simulated proof
Of her chamber to make Posthumus mad,
By wounding his belief in her renown
With averting notes and this her bracelet –
O cunning, how I got it – and, some marks
Of secret on her person. He could not then
But think her bond of marriage was quite cracked.

POSTHUMUS still hooded and bound attacks GIACOMO.

POSTHUMUS: You! You Roman fiend! And me, murderer,
Villain! O, give me cord, or knife, or poison,
Some upright justicer! You, king, send out
For torturers ingenious. I am Posthumus.

PISANIA takes off his hood.

GIACOMO and IMOGEN and CYMBELINE recognise him.

He looks at CYMBELINE.

I killed your daughter.

He looks at PISANIA.

                     Villain-like, I lie –
I caused this lesser villain to do it.

	Spit, and throw stones, cast hell upon me, set
	The dogs of the street to bay me: every villain
	Be called Posthumus. Imogen; my life!
	O, Imogen, Imogen, Imogen!
IMOGEN:	Peace, my husband! Hear, hear-
POSTHUMUS:	You scornful boy, would you have a play of this?

He head butts her. She falls.

He goes to stamp on her but PISANIA pulls him away.

GUIDERIUS goes for POSTHUMUS but BELARIUS pulls him back,

PISANIA: Posthumus! You never killed Imogen.
'Til now!

She dives down to IMOGEN and takes her face in her hands.

        Imogen.

IMOGEN stands and is dazed.

IMOGEN: Does the world go round?
How come these staggers on me?

POSTHUMUS: Imogen.

CYMBELINE: If this be so, then God does mean to strike me
To death with mortal joy.

IMOGEN turns on PISANIA.

IMOGEN: Get from my sight!
You gave me poison, dangerous woman. Go!

CYMBELINE: The tune of Imogen!

PISANIA: God strike me, if
That box I gave you was not thought by me
A precious thing: I had it from the queen.

IMOGEN: It poisoned me.

CORNELIUS: One thing the queen confessed.
Which must approve you honest: 'If Pisania
Have,' said she, 'given Imogen that confection
Which I gave her for medicine, she is served
As I would serve a rat.' Have you taken it?

IMOGEN: Yes I did, for I was dead.

GUIDERIUS: Fidele!

IMOGEN goes over to GUIDERIUS and ARVIRAGUS and the all hold each other.

CYMBELINE: My flesh, my child! Will you not speak to me?

IMOGEN breaks from GUIDERIUS and ARVIRAGUS and looks at CYMBELINE.

BELARIUS goes to GUIDERIUS and ARVIRAGUS.

BELARIUS: *(Signs and speaks)*
Though you did love this youth, I blame you not:
You had a motive for it.

CYMBELINE: My tears that fall
Prove holy water on you! Imogen,
My wife is dead.

IMOGEN: I am sorry for that.

CYMBELINE: Her son is gone, we know not how nor where.

PISANIA: On Imogen's missing, he swore to me,
If I revealed not which way she was gone,
It was my instant death. I had a feigned
Letter of Posthumus which directed him
To seek her near to Milford –

GUIDERIUS: Let me end the story: I slew him there.

CYMBELINE: I would not your good deeds should from my lips
Pluck a hard sentence. Now valiant youth,
Deny it!

GUIDERIUS: I did it. Cut off his head!

IMOGEN: *(To POSTHUMUS.)* That headless man I thought it had
been you.

GUIDERIUS: And am right glad he is not standing here
To tell this tale of mine.

CYMBELINE: You are condemned.
Bind the offender.

CYMBELINE's people move on GUIDERIUS. There is a struggle.

You're dead.

BELARIUS: Cymbeline,
This man is better than the man he slew.

IMOGEN: Let his arms alone.

BELARIUS: And Polydore has
More of you merited than a band of Clotens
Had ever scar for.

CYMBELINE: Why, old soldier,
Will you undo the worth you are unpaid for,
By tasting of our wrath?

BELARIUS: My sons, I must,
For my own part, unfold a dangerous speech,
Though, maybe, well for you.

ARVIRAGUS: *(Signs.)*   Your danger's ours.

CYMBELINE notices the signing.

BELARIUS: You had a friend was called Belarius.

CYMBELINE: What of him? He is a banished traitor.

BELARIUS hold his arms out wide.

BELARIUS: He it is that has
Assumed this age; indeed a banished man;
I know not how a traitor.

CYMBELINE: Take him now:
The whole world shall not save him.

CYMBELINE's people go for BELARIUS.

IMOGEN: Not too hot.

BELARIUS: First pay me for the nursing of your sons.

CYMBELINE: Nursing of my sons!

BELARIUS: They call me father
And think they are my sons, but are not mine.
They are your issue, Cymbeline.

CYMBELINE: How, mine?

BELARIUS: So sure as you your father's. I, old Morgan,
Am that Belarius whom you sometime banished.
My treason, was your invention. Only
My suffering was real. Beaten for loyalty,
Excited me to steal these gentle boys –

For such and so they are. These twenty years
I've trained them up. Those arts they have as I
Could put into them.

He sobs. IMOGEN goes to him.

Here are your sons again; and I must lose
Two of the sweetest companions in the world.

IMOGEN: My gentle brothers.

CYMBELINE: I lost my children:
If these be they, I know not how to wish
A pair of worthier sons.

BELARIUS: Be pleased awhile.

He indicates to GUIDERIUS.

This gentleman, whom I call Polydore,
As yours, is true Guiderius.

He pulls ARVIRAGUS towards CYMBELINE.

                    Cadwal –

CYMBELINE: My younger son, *(Speaks and slowly signs.)* Arviragus.

BELARIUS: This is he.

ARVIRAGUS: *(Signs.)* You can sign?

CYMBELINE: *(Signs.)* Somehow, I remember how we signed when
you were a child.

BELARIUS: *(Signs and speaks.)* It was wise nature's end for this to be
His evidence now.

CYMBELINE: *(Speaks and signs the odd word he can remember.)*
                    So, now what, am I
A mother to the birth of three? Never mother
Rejoiced deliverance more.

IMOGEN: Gentle brothers
Never say I am not truest speaker:
You called me brother, when I was but your
Sister; I you brothers, when you were so indeed.

CYMBELINE: Did you ever meet?

ARVIRAGUS: *(Signs.)* Yes. When she was a boy, Fidele.

GUIDERIUS: And at first meeting loved; continued so,
Until we thought he died.

CYMBELINE: Imogen.
Why fled you from the court?

Indicates to BELARIUS, GUIDERIUS and ARVIRAGUS.
How first met them?
And when came you to serve our Roman captive?

IMOGEN: Good Caius, I will yet do you service.

*She goes to let him down. CYMBELINE nods to some of his people
and they take over from her.*

POSTHUMUS goes over to IMOGEN and takes hold of her arm.

CYMBELINE: See, Posthumus anchors on Imogen,

IMOGEN turns to look at POSTHUMUS.

And she, like harmless lightning, throws her eye
On him –

IMOGEN: You made this wager? I'm your wife.

POSTHUMUS: Is it enough that I am sorry?

IMOGEN: No!
Strike me again but do not say such things.

POSTHUMUS: My conscience is more fettered than my wrists.

IMOGEN: That Pisania should have murdered me
Upon your command. She kill me? My blood?
Her own hands take away my life. Why? Why?

POSTHUMUS: My fury came not out of weak surmises
But from evidence. I thought this Roman,
In an hour or less, had found no opposition.

IMOGEN: This you think makes good to me all that you betrayed?
And I false? You did suffer Giacomo,
Slight thing, to taint your nobler heart
And brain with needless jealousy? How? Why?

GIACOMO throws himself on his knees in front of POSTHUMUS.

GIACOMO My heavy conscience sinks my knee. Take my life,
Which I so often owe. But your ring first,

And here the bracelet of the truest wife
That ever swore her faith.

IMOGEN: Kneel not to him.

She kicks him to the floor.

Kneel not to him. I have the power to
Spare you, the power to forgive you: live,
And deal with others better.

CYMBELINE: Nobly doomed.

IMOGEN turns back to POSTHUMUS – she points at him.

IMOGEN: *(To CYMBELINE.)* Father, here's
The soldier that did company these three
And that so nobly fought. Well he becomes
The grace and the favours of Cymbeline.

CYMBELINE: We'll learn the generosity of our
Imogen. Pardon is the word to all.

He turns to BELARIUS.

You are my brother; so I'll hold you ever.

IMOGEN runs and jumps up on POSTHUMUS – she hugs his neck.

Everyone watching as she just hangs from him.

IMOGEN: Why did you throw your wedded lady from you?
Think that I have you in a lock; and now
Throw me again.

POSTHUMUS: Hang there like fruit, my soul,
Till the tree die!

Everyone watches them for a time.

CYMBELINE: Well, publish we this peace
To all. Caius, let us set forward,
A Roman and a Briton together,
And through London we will march as friends.
Our peace we'll ratify, seal it with feasts.
Set on there!

Apart from IMOGEN and POSTHUMUS all start to move away.

Never did a war cease,
Before bloody hands were washed, with such a peace.

He leaves with the others.
IMOGEN hangs from POSTHUMUS' neck.

END